FENG SHUI
for Healing

FENG SHUI

for

Healing

A Step-by-Step Guide to
Improving Wellness in
Your Home Sanctuary

RODIKA TCHI

ROCKRIDGE
PRESS

Interior and Cover Designer: Peatra Jariya
Art Producer: Karen Beard
Editor: Rochelle Torke
Production Manager: Riley Hoffman
Production Editor: Melissa Edeburn

Photography ©iStock; except pg.v © Stocksy/MaaHoo Studio; pg.37 ©Stocksy/Santi Nunez; pg. 38 © Lucia Loiso; pg.75 © Stocksy/Aleksandar Novoselski

ISBN: Print 978-1-64152-804-7 | eBook 978-1-64152-805-4

R0

To life
and love
in all its
endless forms.

CONTENTS

INTRODUCTION

The world that we live in
is beautiful, inspiring, and full
of endless wonder. It can be a
sanctuary of sacred beauty,
creativity, joy, and healing.

Our world is also one of enormous complexity. Whereas the outer world, with its constant turbulence, is mostly out of our control, there are two other worlds that we can control—our inner world and our home.

Creating a powerful and supportive home sanctuary is the essence of feng shui. Since ancient times, the Chinese practitioners who developed and refined this practice have understood that our homes can strengthen and nourish us no matter what is happening in the outside world. The energy in your home directly influences your health and well-being on all levels. It can also amplify the vibrancy and depth of your inner world.

Creating your own harmonious home is not only healing and empowering for you and your family, but it also contributes to healing the outer world. The more harmonious and happy homes we create, the more we shift the balance in the outer world from chaos to harmony.

The health and well-being movement is reaching a wider audience than ever before. Energetic practices that were once relatively unknown, such as meditation, Qigong, and Tai Chi, are now taught in schools. But we still have a long way to go in terms of understanding how the energy in our space influences our well-being.

Taking care of your health involves balancing many factors, such as good nutrition, proper exercise, satisfying relationships, meaningful work, and more. One of the crucial factors in enjoying good health is knowing how to receive support from your immediate surroundings—in other words, how to create a happy and healthy home that is there for you, no matter what.

I am here to help you achieve that with the ancient art and science of feng shui. Let's begin by learning more about it together.

CHAPTER

1

There are few words in any language that are more powerful and more widely used than the word *home*. A happy and healthy home is a home where love is present, because love brings the energy of healing, connection, and joy that is crucial for one's health. When we say that someone "feels like home to me," we mean that person carries a safe and accepting energy of love.

HOME:
The Foundation of
Health and Happiness

Did you know that in ancient times, Chinese doctors always asked their patients about their homes? This was part of establishing the right diagnosis and the best treatment. That's how important your home is!

In Western culture, we don't value a harmonious home in the way that Eastern culture does. We place importance on our home's style and location and whether it satisfies the basic needs of our family members. We rarely talk about its energy and how it feels and instead focus on the more superficial levels of look and functionality. Although these criteria are important, they are not what deeply nurtures and sustains our well-being.

What, then, is most important for your well-being at home? The answer is in the energy of your space. I know the word *energy* sounds elusive, but I am sure you have seen many modest homes that felt very happy and nurturing, and strikingly beautiful homes that felt cold and lonely. That feeling in any space is its energy.

The ancient art and science of feng shui makes the unconscious in your home conscious. It regards your home as the foundation of your health and happiness. Feng shui gives you numerous tools to create a home that is a sanctuary of joy and well-being.

UNDERSTANDING THE ESSENCE: WHAT IS QI?

The notion of Qi—also known as universal energy—is one of the most fundamental concepts in traditional Chinese healing practices. This vital force is acknowledged in many cultures: The Hindus call it *prana*, the Japanese call it *Ki*, and in the Jewish culture this powerful force is called *ruah*. In the Western world

we acknowledge it by many names that only partially describe it, such as vital energy, power, passion, or vigor.

In brief, Qi is the universal energy that permeates the world around us. Everything from a budding leaf to a mighty mountain is made out of Qi. You might have heard your acupuncturist explaining the flow of Qi via the meridians in the human body, or maybe your Tai Chi or Qigong instructor has a special way of showing how to cultivate the Qi in your body.

ANYA'S STORY

After moving into her sleek new condo on the 20th floor of a high-rise, Anya started experiencing a lot of anxiety. A feng shui consultation revealed that the energy in her home was stark and ungrounded. The kitchen was cold and sterile, and the bedroom felt overly exposed to the outside world due to floor-to-ceiling windows. She had also inadvertently placed a rather melancholic piece of art over the fireplace.

After seeing the home through the feng shui lens, Anya carefully incorporated enhancements that trans-formed how she felt there. She added colorful appliances, vibrant art, fresh potted herbs, and a big bowl of fruit to the kitchen. Beautiful window treatments softened the energy in her bedroom, creating privacy and darkening the room at night. She replaced the moody art over the fireplace with a big mirror in a thick wooden frame. A few vibrant, tall plants, ambient lighting, many colorful cushions, and a cozy rug in the living room made the space feel like home. With just a few feng shui changes focused on grounding the energy, Anya finally started feeling safer and more peaceful.

A well-balanced flow of Qi nourishes each organ and system in your body, promoting health and vitality, whereas a blocked or stagnant Qi promotes illness. Feng shui is one of the many techniques that help strengthen and increase the quality of Qi in the body. It is part of a toolbox that contains breathing exercises, meditation, acupuncture, and more. The quality of your personal Qi on many levels—from physical to mental to emotional—is largely determined by the overall Qi in your home.

WHAT IS FENG SHUI?

One of the most precise definitions of feng shui—and the one that I like the most—is "acupuncture of the space." Feng shui studies your home as if it were your body and knows how to open up its Qi flow so that your own energy can move freely and smoothly. The quality of Qi and its flow in your home is one of the defining factors in how your space can support your well-being.

Feng shui originated over 5,000 years ago in imperial China and for a long time was kept a secret practice used only for privileged members of society. Along with many other healing arts, feng shui was employed to promote the energy of good luck, health, and happiness. Its main goal is to improve the destiny of humans by aligning the energy of a human dwelling with the energy of the great outdoors and to balance the space so it is in harmony with the laws of nature. This aligning and balancing is achieved using a variety of tools, cures, and calculations—many of which you will find in this book.

As with any ancient body of knowledge, many schools of thought have developed over time that either apply feng shui in slightly different ways or are focused on different aspects of feng shui. For example, there are feng shui schools that calculate the auspicious dates for specific events, schools that focus on the physical aspect of the environment while applying spiritual meditations and rituals, and schools that focus mostly on the astrological aspects of the house. All of these contribute to better understanding the art of feng shui.

USING FENG SHUI FOR HEALING AND VITALITY

Feng shui is considered a healing art, along with traditional Chinese medicine, acupuncture, medical Qigong, Tai Chi, Gua Sha, and many other modalities. One of the main uses of feng shui is to create an environment that exudes vitality, health, happiness, and well-being. Even though this idea sounds easy, there are many complex layers that one needs to go through in transforming a home into an oasis of healing and happy energy. However, going into complex feng shui layers without first addressing the very necessary basics will not work; a good foundation has to be created first.

Some people become concerned with esoteric and advanced feng shui considerations, such as specific calculations related to when the house was built. However, there are far more basic elements to feng shui that often get overlooked, such as a good flow of fresh air or enough natural light. You might have all the calculations in place, but if you haven't addressed the flow of your space, the symbolism of objects in your home, and other basic but essential elements, you could be wasting your time. There are specific levels to follow for successful feng shui work in order to improve one's health and vitality. I will guide you through the main steps.

HOW THIS BOOK CAN HELP YOU

You've probably picked up this book because you're already sensitive to how your home environment affects you and you're sincerely interested in creating a space that will support and nourish your health and well-being. I will share many feng shui health tips and "feng shui cures," which are edits to your living space that produce positive effects.

I'll show you how to create a nurturing home that increases your vitality, supports healing work, and assists you with specific health goals. My tips are not theoretical but come from my deep study of various feng shui schools as well as direct observations drawn from over 19 years of feng shui consulting work. I'll share stories from my clients and give you simple but powerful suggestions for enhancing the energy in your home and your body.

In addition to traditional and modern feng shui practices, you'll find tips for moving blocked energy in your body and life. Mindful pauses throughout the book are designed to help you slow down, connect with Qi energy through breath work, and soothe your mind with affirmations. Centering yourself in this way can ground you and prepare you to approach your home with energy and awareness.

I hope you'll find this book to be a longtime ally as you care for your home and yourself.

MINDFUL PAUSE

4-SQUARE BREATH

Sit quietly.

Draw your mind inward.
Relax your face,
chest, and belly.

Breathe in for four counts,
hold for four counts, and
breathe out for four counts.

Repeat six to ten times.

Read the affirmation
out loud three times.

AFFIRMATION

I can create a nourishing home
no matter where I go.

CHAPTER

2

In the feng shui language, your home is a direct reflection of your inner world. A good feng shui consultant can find out a lot about you just by seeing your home. From the floor plan and the way you arranged the furniture to the images and colors (or lack of them) or the specific patterns and symbols in your art, textiles, and other decor items—they all reveal the workings of your inner world. Your likes, dislikes, desires, worries, and dreams are all expressed in your home for those who know how to read the symbolism and energy of a space.

READ YOUR HOME, Know Yourself

The good news about feng shui is that it helps you unblock the energy in your home, your life, and your physical vitality. Through your feng shui work, you can enable the fresh and harmonious flow of Qi, improving your own energy and attracting more of what you desire in your life.

It is helpful to know the signs of blocked Qi as well as signs of happy, flowing Qi. By cultivating this sensitivity, you'll know when it's time to do a little feng shui tune-up in your space using the tips described in this book. You'll know the quality of the energy in your own home and how to enhance it to feel the way you want to feel.

Have you ever experienced a feeling of harmony and a quiet sense of joy upon entering a specific space? These feelings are transformative. You find yourself becoming lighter, and there is a sweet and nourishing sense of enjoyment. You completely forget that only minutes ago, you were stressed out or tired. You feel relaxed and gently energized at the same time. In other words, you feel good! How can this be possible just by walking into a room? What makes it so magical?

When the space looks beautiful and well decorated, it all makes sense to you, but how about a place that looks modest with nothing impressive about it? What creates that really good feeling when there is nothing really obvious to point to?

By the same token, most of us have experienced feeling a bit uneasy, if not anxious, upon entering a space. When this feeling is caused by something as obvious as clutter or not enough ventilation or natural light, then our experience is easy to understand. However, what if on the surface both spaces looked very similar? What would be the reason for feeling joyful and energized in one versus anxious and even sad in another?

This variation all comes down to the mysterious and powerful flow of Qi, or universal energy, in any given space. Knowing how to create a good Qi flow and how to nourish and strengthen it is what good feng shui is all about. Making your home Qi work for you and support your goals is an art you can easily learn; it only takes a bit of practice and discipline.

In order to support your health and well-being, the Qi in your home has to be fresh and full of vitality, and flow with ease. A simple test to see if your home Qi is good for you or not is to sense how you feel right upon entering your home. Do you feel peaceful, calm, and happy, or do agitation and restlessness come to you? Do you feel tired all of a sudden, or is there a gentle boost of good, loving energy enveloping your whole being?

It is best to do this Qi checkup when you come home after being away for a few days so that your energy is slightly detached from your home and you can read it with more objectivity. It is also helpful to ask a close friend how he or she feels in your home. We get used to our environments because they mirror us and we mirror them, so it is important to do your best to assess the quality of your home Qi accurately.

Are there specific signs that show when the Qi in your home is working for or against you? Can you easily tell? Absolutely! Here are the signs that your home Qi is working for you as well as the signs that your home Qi flow and quality need to be corrected. A good flow and quality of Qi can make all the difference in one's life!

SIGNS OF HAPPY HOME QI

Here are the signs that your home Qi is happy and working hard to create goodness in your life.

When your home Qi is working for you:

- You feel at ease and happy with yourself.
- Your life seems to flow well, and even if you encounter setbacks, they tend to be resolved quickly.
- You have a good relationship with yourself and those around you.
- You are in good health.
- You have a happy and satisfying intimate relationship, and your family life tends to be happy.
- There is a sense of exploration and wonder in your life.
- There is laughter and a sense of joy in your home.
- You feel peaceful and calm, and when things don't go the way you want, you feel okay about it.
- You feel grateful for your life.

SIGNS OF STAGNANT OR BLOCKED QI

Here are the signs that your home Qi flow and quality need to be corrected because you and your home Qi are not in harmony.

When your home Qi is working against you:

- You tend to feel irritable and constantly look to improve your life rather than enjoy it.
- Your relationships tend to have a lot of turmoil, or they end abruptly.
- You are not happy with your career, and you struggle financially.
- You dream of a happy intimate relationship and do not understand why you fail to attract a good partner.
- Your health fluctuates dramatically.
- You often feel low in energy and leave the projects you dream about for later.
- Boredom and lack of enthusiasm are states you are used to.
- You feel isolated in your house and in your life.
- You are not enjoying the present and would rather think of the past or get lost in an imaginary future.
- No matter how hard you try, accomplishing your goals and dreams seems to elude you.

MINDFUL
PAUSE

4-7-8 YOGA BREATH

Sit quietly.

Draw your mind inward.
Relax your face,
chest, and belly.

Breathe in for a count of four.

Hold for a count of seven.

Breathe out gently
for a count of eight.

Repeat six to ten times.

Read the affirmation
out loud three times.

AFFIRMATION

I always take time to listen to the
soft voice of my heart.

Our home environment reflects the state of our energy. It mirrors back to us our fears, desires, insecurities, hopes, and dreams.

LOOK INTO THE MIRROR OF YOUR HOME

The whole premise of feng shui is that we are constantly exchanging energy with our immediate surroundings, so our home environment reflects the state of our energy. It mirrors back to us our fears, desires, insecurities, hopes, and dreams, all in plain view for those who know how to read the space.

Things such as clutter, overstuffed closets, dark rooms, chipped paint, or dying plants are hard to overlook, so be sure to pay attention and see why you tolerate this low energy and what feelings it evokes in you. In a way, feng shui can serve as powerful therapy—especially when decluttering—because it will mirror back to you all you prefer not to look at.

It will also honestly reflect things that you are not consciously aware of, such as obvious contradictions between what you say you want and how you actually express those desires. I remember working with a client in her early 30s who wanted to attract a life partner. She had quite a few solitary images in her bedroom, often made from cold, gray stone. There were frames on her wall with images such as one flower, one heart, one candle, and an empty vase. The look was aesthetically pleasing but still very lonely. There was a sense of sadness, separation, and aloofness about them. So even though she said she wanted to attract a partner, on a subconscious level there was a lot of resistance to it.

During our consultation she agreed to take these items out of the bedroom, but as we continued our work in other rooms of the house, she took them right back to her bedroom. I did not insist on leaving those images out of the bedroom as she obviously needed to take her time. The best I could do was clearly point out the dissonance between her desire and her actual behavior.

Of course, your home also mirrors all the goodness in your life. The beauty, the flow, and the harmony that you create are always there to support you. The happy plants around the house,

the healing crystals, the art that evokes joy and happiness, and the little touches here and there that express a sense of love and nourishment are all good testimony to the powerful energy work that you achieve with feng shui.

Let's use feng shui to assess your space. The first assessment is basic and easy to do. Simply notice everything around you and what kind of mood it creates. Look at your house and see what feelings different areas of your home and different decor items evoke in your heart. What do you like, and what you do not like? If you do not like something, why do you keep it?

The next level, which you will learn soon, is to look at specific feng shui areas that represent specific aspects of your life and understand the deeper patterns. You will find out exactly how to do that in chapter 3 (page 25).

HOME-STUDY TABLE

The chart on the following pages can help you decode the feng shui meaning of most common decor solutions in one's home. The first step is always to ask if you are happy with the specific colors, images, and decor in your space. The second step is to see what feelings or desires they evoke in you.

For example, you might find yourself gravitating toward images of butterflies and realize you have this image in various photos, textiles, and even your kitchenware. Ask yourself about the specific association you have with this symbol, because obviously your energy is craving it and needs it. This process is very personal and does not have to conform with the traditional meaning of the image, even though looking up the traditional meaning of any given symbol can help you delve deeper into your own subconscious associations.

Next comes the feng shui interpretation of your inquiry, which is followed by specific action you might want to take prompted by the language of your decor choices. In the example with the butterflies, you might have personal associations with the carefree and happy summer fun of chasing butterflies with your now deceased brother. Traditionally, butterflies speak to metamorphosis and transformation into freedom, grace, and beauty. In this specific case, there is an additional deep layer of grieving that might need to be addressed in order for you to heal and thrive. A good feng shui home decor study will explore the personal energy of the owner—his or her dreams, concerns, and fears—along with the overall feng shui energy of any given item.

Here is a simple feng shui chart that can help you understand the language of your choices and how this language can prompt specific changes to improve your life.

OBSERVATION	PERSONAL ASSOCIATION	FENG SHUI INTERPRETATION	INSPIRED ACTION
Many images of birds around the house	Birds remind me of summers spent at my grandmother's cottage, where I felt free and happy. I feel constricted in my life, so these images help me feel free and inspired.	In feng shui, birds represent the freedom of choice.	I feel the call for more freedom in my life, and I want to explore it even in small ways that are possible right now. I commit to taking new paths to work, attempting new hikes, and trying short trips to exercise my freedom of choice.
Cluttered closets	I feel safer when my closets are full of many things; it gives me a sense of stability and grounding, safety, and even abundance. Looking at all I have in my closet makes me feel more secure and even protected.	Clutter is always a sign of stagnant and blocked energy. More often than not, clutter symbolizes the reluctance to deal with one's fears and anxieties. In closets especially, clutter is often related to our inner sense of self, self-esteem, and self-love.	I need to take time to at least organize all this clutter and decide if I need all the items by looking at each one of them. If it turns out that I do, I need to organize them properly, so my closet is busy and full but not cluttered.
Many mirrors around the house	Mirrors make me feel fresh. They remind me of things like clear water, morning light, and openness.	Mirrors are a classical feng shui Water element cure, which means they bring the energy of water. They also expand the space and bring more light to it. However, too many mirrors in one's home weaken its energy. A good home needs the uninterrupted energetic solidity of walls.	I need to undertake activities that will freshen, open up, and expand my energy. I can do more swimming and kayaking and maybe look into something gentle, like Qigong. I would love to have more meaningful, close relationships where I can open up more and be supported as well as support others. I need more expansion and more growth in my life. I need to come out of my box.

OBSERVATION	PERSONAL ASSOCIATION	FENG SHUI INTERPRETATION	INSPIRED ACTION
Single-figure images	I feel supported when I see the images of beautiful single people. I feel understood and somehow not so alone anymore.	Having many solitary images around one's home, especially if the owner is single, can become an energetic impediment to finding a good intimate relationship.	I need to understand myself more. I need to connect to more people in my life, see how different personalities feel to me, and consider how I can create lasting relationships. If I want to be in a romantic relationship but have been single for a while, I need to look at what is stopping me from enjoying love with an intimate partner.
Too many collections, too much furniture	I feel cocooned and cozy when I have tons of stuff around me. I feel like I am in a fortress and feel very protected. No care in the world can touch me when I'm here.	A house that has too many items—be it furniture, collections, or any other decor pieces—can create a sense of hiding from the world. A good feng shui house needs a balance of protection and openness so that new things can flow into one's life.	I might be willing to look into my need to hide and feel protected. I would love a good change in my life, but I also love to be in comfort and to feel safe. I will try to let go of some things and see how the openness makes me feel.

MINDFUL
PAUSE

4-7-8 YOGA BREATH

Sit quietly.

Draw your mind inward.
Relax your face,
chest, and belly.

Breathe in for a count of four.

Hold for a count of seven.

Breathe out gently
for a count of eight.

Repeat six to ten times.

Read the affirmation
out loud three times.

AFFIRMATION

To calm myself, I need only my breath
and the earth beneath my feet.

CHAPTER

3

There are many feng shui tools that can help balance the energy of your home and promote vibrant health and a happy sense of well-being. The feng shui *bagua*, or the energy map of the space, is the main tool used in this process. Applied correctly, it shows you how specific areas of your home are connected to specific areas of your life, thus allowing you to make the desired changes.

Universal VITALITY BOOSTERS

Along with the bagua, feng shui offers a wide variety of techniques and cures to help balance and boost the energy in your home. Don't worry about being perfect; some of these tools can be applied even without knowing the bagua of your home. However, most feng shui health cures work best when they are placed in specific feng shui areas connected to the energy of health and vitality.

In order to avoid any confusion, let me clarify right away that there are two different baguas—feng shui energy maps—that are used to determine the feng shui map of your home. Both baguas are powerful. They both work and both bring positive results. The main thing to know is that it is best not to use both at the same time.

I want to guide you on how to use the so-called Western bagua, which is a simple and practical way to start applying feng shui in your life. The other bagua, called the Classical bagua, requires somewhat complex feng shui compass readings and calculations, so we will not be using it here.

The feng shui bagua we will work with is a grid that is easily superimposed over the floor plan of your home. You will need to draw your home floor plan if you do not have one from your architect, realtor, or city hall.

The Feng Shui Bagua
You can find out how specific areas of your life are represented in specific areas of your home.

MONEY & ABUNDANCE	FAME & REPUTATION	LOVE & MARRIAGE
HEALTH & FAMILY	HEART CENTER	CHILDREN & CREATIVITY
SPIRITUAL GROWTH	CAREER & LIFE PATH	HELPFUL PEOPLE

An example floor plan for a home.

Align the bagua map with the front door of your home to see how different aspects of your life are mirrored in that area.
When you face challenges or feel stuck, look for clutter, an excess of furniture, or negative imagery in the area of your home associated with the challenging part of your life.

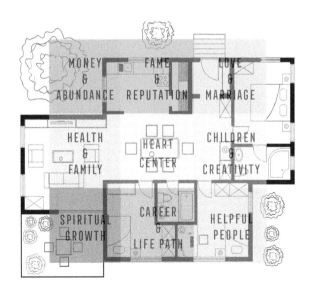

As you can see, the feng shui bagua has nine squares or rectangles, all defined by the ancient masters as important areas of one's life. One specific feng shui bagua area—located on the mid-left portion of the bagua grid—is directly related to your health and well-being. Another very important area for the health and vitality of people living in the home is the center of the home, also called the heart center or Yin Yang point. It is very important to keep your center clean, open, and clear, as this is where all the other bagua areas draw energy from.

The way to apply the bagua is really simple: Align the bottom portion of the bagua with the front door of your home.

PROTECT AND ENHANCE YOUR VITALITY

There are many feng shui tips you can apply in your home in order to improve your health and well-being. Let's start with the most fundamental ones.

THE ESSENTIAL ELEMENTS

What are the feng shui elements, and why are they important? According to the ancient Taoist masters, the feng shui elements are the main expression of Qi and are the building blocks of our universe. Defined as Water, Wood, Fire, Earth, and Metal, these elements are present everywhere, including in our personal energy. The full expression of these elements is very important for a healthy home, so feng shui places a big emphasis on specific decor items and objects that bring the quality of a needed element into your home.

Each element offers a specific quality of energy, and we need all five elements for our health and well-being. For example, the Fire element brings passion and vitality, while Metal enhances focus and determination. When a space lacks the presence of a specific feng shui element, it becomes energetically weak and cannot support your well-being. Each element is expressed in specific decor items that bring its presence into your home. Let's look at the elements one by one and learn how you can bring each one into your home.

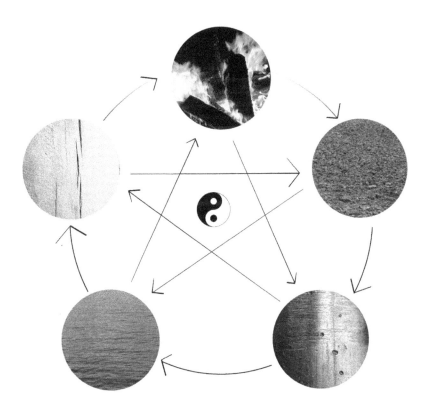

Water

The Water element is vital for humans' health. Without water, there is no life on Earth; without the Water feng shui element in one's home, there is a lack of vitality, calm, and abundance. The most popular cures to bring this important element are

- Fountains
- Water bowls
- Mirrors
- Images of water
- Wavy shapes
- Blue and black colors

Wood

The Wood element is the element of growth, health, and vitality. Trees—the main expression of the Wood element—clean the air we breathe and provide shade and shelter. When a home lacks the Wood element, it can easily become cluttered and imbalanced, to the point of feeling suffocating. A balanced Wood element brings a sense of health and well-being to any space. The main expressions of the Wood element are

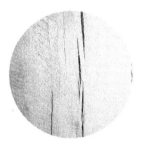

- Plants
- Images of lush landscapes
- Furniture made from natural wood
- Green and brown colors

Fire

The Fire element is certainly very important as life on Earth is maintained by the warmth and creativity of the sun, the main expression of this element. Similarly, the energy in your home is nourished by the presence of a good Fire feng shui element. The main expressions of this element are

- Real fire, such as candles and fireplaces
- Images of fire
- Triangle and star shapes
- Red, magenta, pink, purple, and orange colors

Earth

The Earth element is also very important because it brings the energy of stability, grounding, and centeredness. If you notice that these qualities are lacking in your daily life, use the feng shui cures of the Earth feng shui element to bring yourself back to balance. The most popular expressions of this element are

- Earthenware objects
- Terra-cotta tiles and pots
- Clay pots filled with sand
- Images of vast landscapes, such as deserts
- Square shapes
- Crystals and rocks
- Sandy and earthy colors

Metal

The Metal element is the most misunderstood in terms of its importance in the home—it is not the items made from metal (which are still a good feng shui cure) but the energy of the Metal element that the home needs. This element is expressed in a quality of energy that is crisp, clear, clean, sharp, and spacious.

Metal energy cuts through without leaving room for any doubt, hesitation, or procrastination. This means a lack of clutter. Typical decor items that express the Metal element include

- Items made from metal or with metal finishes
- Square and circle shapes
- White and gray colors

Now that you know the elements and their main expressions in decor items, where do you place them? How do you decorate with elements for good feng shui? For the best placement of the cures that represent specific elements, it is good to know which areas are welcoming for a specific element and which ones would rather avoid it. We'll cover placement later in the chapter.

BREATH AND LIGHT

Even though it is widely known that fresh air and good natural light are great for one's well-being, they are often disregarded when it comes to the home. I have been in many homes with stale air in every room and with most natural light blocked, even when there was plenty available. It is important to know that both air and light provide complex nutrition for our bodies. Remembering to open windows often in order to let in fresh air and natural light is very important for your vitality and your sense of well-being.

In cases when there is no possibility for fresh air circulation or natural light use (such as in a basement or a room with no windows), it is important to use skillful tools to satisfy these requirements. The best way to create fresh, clean air is to use an air purifier, an ultrasonic aromatherapy diffuser, or both.

The need for fresh, clean air is quite self-explanatory, but the need for natural light is easily misunderstood. According to the pioneering research of Dr. John Ott, natural light is very important energetic nutrition for the human body. This nutrition is measured in units called lux. For example, the level of lux outdoors on a clear, sunny day is about 10,000, whereas indoors it can be as little as 50. The more lux in your home, the better, so be mindful about opening blinds, curtains, and other window treatments in order to maximize the light in your home.

PLANTS TO THE RESCUE

Using plants—specifically, air-purifying plants—is an excellent feng shui health cure that brings numerous physical, emotional, and even mental benefits. In feng shui, most cures bring the energy of specific elements; in the case of plants, the energy they bring is of the Wood element. Which plants should you use? Are there any specific plants to avoid? The best plants to use are air-purifying plants. Here are 12 of the most popular:

- Peace lily
- English ivy
- Dwarf palm
- Spider plant
- Rubber plant
- Boston fern
- Areca palm
- Dracaena Jenny Craig
- Weeping fig
- Snake plant
- Aloe vera
- Bamboo palm

As for plants to avoid, the only rule is to avoid dead or sick plants. You want your plants to exude vitality and strong nature Qi, not stale, dead energy.

A wise guideline when it comes to decorating your home with plants is to avoid plants with sharp leaves in your bedroom, such as the yucca tree or snake plant. This does not mean that these plants are bad feng shui; their strong protective energy is just not suited for the bedroom. Instead, they can be an excellent choice close to the front door or in the living room.

The best overall placement of plants is in the feng shui areas that *love* the Wood element: the Health & Family, Money & Abundance, and Fame & Reputation areas.

The main area to *avoid* having many plants is the Career & Life Path area because of the clash of elements (Wood weakens the Water element needed in this area). Other areas to limit the display of big plants are the Love & Marriage area, the Heart Center, and the Spiritual Growth area.

ARRANGING YOUR SPACE TO SUPPORT WELLNESS

Would a red couch be good feng shui for your Career & Life Path area? How about a fountain in the Children & Creativity area? The answers to these questions are easy when you know which element is needed in a specific bagua area. Let's start with the areas that benefit from decorating with a specific feng shui element and then explore the bagua areas where specific decor should be limited.

The Fire element decor brings passionate, vital energy to any area. In the Fame & Reputation area, it lights up your inner fire and helps attract success. In the Love & Marriage area, Fire helps reignite and keep passion alive, and in the Spiritual Growth area, it fuels your search for truth. The Fire element is also very important in the Heart Center because it brings warmth and openness to the whole house.

The Earth element brings a supportive and nourishing foundation to the Health & Family area and provides stability in the Money & Abundance and Love & Marriage areas. It gives depth and support to allow the expansion of your creativity in the Children & Creativity area. The Earth element encourages you to seek the right support in the Helpful People and Spiritual Growth areas. This element is also important in the Heart Center and Health & Family area because of its energy of nourishment, support, and unconditional acceptance.

Metal element decor brings the necessary clarity and structure to create good energy in the Children & Creativity and

Helpful People areas. The sharpness of the Metal element is also very supportive of your Career & Life Path area.

Decorating with the Water element brings freshness and vitality to the Health & Family area, a good flow of prosperity to the Money & Abundance area, and a flow of ease and success in your Career & Life Path area.

The Wood element is essential for the vitality of the Health & Family area and for the strength of prosperity in the Money & Abundance area. A strong Wood element in the Fame & Reputation area provides the energetic support to be seen and progress on your path.

It is also important to know where *not* to place many cures of a specific element, to prevent an energetic imbalance or weakness in the area. For example, if you have too many Fire element decor items in your Health & Family area, you risk creating the energy of depletion and burnout, so a red feature wall in this area is not a good idea. If you place a big blue couch or a fountain in the Fame & Reputation area, you will be weakening the brightness of your fiery and creative energy.

Here are specific areas to avoid placing specific element cures:

- A strong Fire feng shui element cure can considerably drain the energy in the following areas: Health & Family, Money & Abundance, Career & Life Path, Children & Creativity, Helpful People.
- Limit Earth element cures in the Fame & Reputation and Career & Life Path areas in order to avoid stagnation and blockages.
- The Metal element should be limited in the Health & Family and Money & Abundance areas, as it can weaken the well-being and wealth of the family.
- The Water element puts down the fire and the passion needed in the Fame & Reputation and Love & Marriage areas. It also depletes the energy needed in the Children & Creativity and Helpful People areas.

- Avoid a strong Wood element in the Love & Marriage area, as it weakens the stability of the marriage. The Wood element should also be limited in the Health & Family and Spiritual Growth bagua areas.

STRENGTHEN YOUR HEALTH WITH SMART FENG SHUI

To maintain high levels of well-being, the energy in your whole home has to be harmonious and balanced. However, as with everything else, there are priorities and areas to focus on first in order to strengthen the energy of health. Here are the main areas connected to your health and vitality that need to be well balanced.

Health & Family

Decorate this bagua area with a variety of cures of the Wood and Water feng shui elements, such as plants, fountains, mirrors, images of water and lush landscapes, and happy family photos. A bit of the Earth feng shui element is good here, too, such as crystals, earthenware pots, or landscape images. The main focus of your feng shui decorating here should be on expressing the energy of family harmony.

Heart Center

The Heart Center of your home is the area from which all other bagua areas draw energy, so it is important to have the best possible energy there whenever you're working on a health or wellness goal. The Heart Center connects to your health because it's directly connected to your heart energy, and the vibration of this area in your house ripples outward, touching all the other baguas.

Place decor items here that express the energy of love, health, and harmony, with various items made from either Fire or Earth feng shui elements. Good examples of such cures are crystals (especially in heart shapes), candles, colorful flowers, or happy family photos. Inspirational quotes and images that speak to your heart are also excellent here.

The main focus of your feng shui decorating in the Heart Center should be on expressing energy and vitality. If you are going through a health crisis, you can display images of your specific cures. For example, if your liver needs cleansing, then images of greens, especially dandelion greens, can be very good feng shui for you.

The Feng Shui Health Trinity: Kitchen, Bathroom, Bedroom

The state of these three rooms in your home is very important for your health and well-being, so be sure to create and maintain the best possible quality of energy there. Clean and clutter free is the beginning of all good feng shui work, followed by specific decor depending on which bagua area any of these rooms falls into. For example, if your kitchen is in the Love & Marriage area, you would be wise to focus on Fire and Earth feng shui element decor, such as a red mixer or terra-cotta pots for your plants.

MINDFUL
PAUSE

4-SQUARE BREATH

Sit quietly.

Draw your mind inward.
Relax your face,
chest, and belly.

Breathe in for four counts.

Hold for four counts.

Breathe out for four counts.

Repeat six to ten times.

Read the affirmation
out loud three times.

AFFIRMATION

I trust my inner healing power.

CHAPTER

4

If you want to improve your vitality, have full access to your own innate healing energy, and enjoy true well-being on a daily basis, you must commit to clearing your clutter. Why would I be so decisive when it comes to clutter? I rarely use the word *must* in any feng shui circumstance. However, if you want to foster healing and enjoy deeper vitality, you just can't have a lot of clutter in your home.

CLUTTER

In the world of energy, clutter is an expression of old, stuck, and discordant energy that can perpetuate itself in your home and in your life. You are energetically connected to every object, seen or unseen, in your living space. An abundance of unused or unloved items, or of objects that have guilt or negativity attached to them, locks emotional currents in your own physical energy body. You then become physically charged in a way that attracts more of that same scattered energy, almost like a magnet with a confused charge. Clutter recreates habitual feelings, behaviors, relationship patterns, repetitive thoughts, attachments, fears, and other forms of low and stuck energy.

Unless you have just moved into your home or are renovating it—in which case the energetic chaos or stagnancy is temporary—know that a cluttered home is an expression of your own energy and can also muffle your self-awareness and conscious decision making. This is where clutter clearing becomes therapy, because it helps you understand many things about yourself that were previously hidden.

Feng shui-wise, it is important to assess which specific bagua areas of your home are cluttered. For example, if there is a lot of clutter in your Career & Life Path area, you might experience blockages in your career growth and maybe even a lack of motivation and vision. If you have clutter in your Love & Marriage area, then you might be experiencing difficulties in your relationship, such as bickering or a feeling that you simply can't connect.

GOT STUFF?

Clutter clearing has become part of feng shui only in recent times. Considering the fact that historically feng shui was mostly a secret art practiced in the abodes of nobility, there is no teaching about decluttering in old feng shui schools.

We speak a lot about clearing clutter in feng shui because there is an epidemic of clutter in most Western homes. Our consumer culture, combined with a lack of time and clarity, provides a perfect breeding ground for clutter in many modern homes. Luckily, this problem has also created a growing industry of organization and storage solutions that are widely available to all who are ready to liberate themselves from the clutches of clutter.

WHY IS IT SO IMPORTANT TO CLEAR CLUTTER?

Remember, clutter is an expression of old, stuck, and discordant energy. This low vibration can perpetuate itself in your home and your life. You are energetically connected to every object, seen or unseen, in your living space. Most unused or unloved

items, as well as objects that have guilt, negativity, or "unfinished business" attached to them, block the flow of energy in your body and therefore deplete your physical energy. You become physically wired in a way that attracts more of that same scattered energy, and you pull in more of the same quality. If your house is overflowing with clutter, that energy is not going to be the highest, and it certainly won't be charged with a clear intention. In this way, clutter in your home tends to create many forms of low and stuck energy.

You can see that pools of stuck energy from clutter are the last thing you need if you're trying to boost your health or shift anything else in your life. If you find yourself feeling tired or depressed when you spend time at home, look no further than your clutter—both the obvious stuff in plain view and the hidden bits tucked here and there.

Clutter drains and scatters the Qi—the very energy you need in order to heal, rejuvenate, and restore yourself. I encourage you to take the presence of clutter in your home seriously and to create a plan to get rid of it in the shortest time possible. There is no need to rush, but there is no need to delay, either. Just commit to it and do it.

There are quite a few systems to help you declutter. I encourage you to first spend some time with your clutter and see what feelings it evokes in you. What feelings do you experience when you think of clearing it all? Do you feel fear? Guilt? Lack of security? Indecisiveness? The process of self-reflection and self-inquiry will help speed up your clutter clearing and bring many helpful insights.

A very simple exercise is to imagine it all gone. Now, how soon will you start creating more? Why? Stay with this *why* for a bit, as it can give you good information. Listen to the sensations in your body, notice your thoughts, and notice your emotions.

Let me share an example from my practice that can help you with your own process. I was working with a long-term client, a lovely lady from a wealthy family who had a lot of creative clutter in her sweet and sunny home office. Her clutter was in different piles of well-being materials, handouts, and samples here and there—all sorts of stuff with no order or proper relationship with its surroundings.

Once we started working, I noticed that the areas that we cleaned were quickly filled again with piles of interesting handouts and materials. This is when I knew we needed to spend more time with the *why* before the actual process of clutter clearing. When you work with the *why*, do not stop until you reach the moment when you realize why there is clutter. Here's how this happened with my client.

Rodika: Janet, let's try to figure out why you have so many handouts, materials, illustrations, and samples everywhere.

Janet: Oh, I just don't have the time to organize it all as I am so busy.

Note: This is a typical answer when you first ask people about clutter.

Rodika: Okay, I see. But look: We cleaned this area completely two weeks ago and now it is getting filled again with the same things.

Janet: I know, I know. I just need more space and time.

Note: This is also a typical answer when you begin questioning.

Rodika: Tell me about all these handouts. Why do you keep them?

Note: When you are coming into the specific content of clutter, you are going deeper.

Janet: Well, I love all this wellness stuff, so I bring it home from all my workshops and travels. I hope that one day I will start applying it!

Rodika: When do you plan to start applying it? When do you think you will have more time?

Janet: Well, I don't really know. I hope soon.

Rodika: What's the feeling that these piles of materials create in you?

Note: After you explore the content, go straight into the feelings, because they express your actual need or desire.

Janet: Worry, but also hope and inspiration. I get a feeling that I am learning and progressing if one day I apply all this info.

Rodika: What do you think can keep the feelings of hope, learning, and progressing, but leave out the worry?

Janet: If I actually do what interests me—all this amazing stuff I keep bringing home info about.

Rodika: Suppose I took them all away. Which ones would you miss the most? Which ones would you want to keep?

Janet: It's the sound healing that so fascinates me. I've got quite a few items to get ready to apply it all soon.

Rodika: Okay, so we can focus on sound healing—prominently display all materials and instruments you already have—and have the rest neatly organized out of sight, yes?

Janet: Yes, sounds good to me!

After we zoomed into the actual reason the clutter was there and the needs and desires behind it, we were able to find a solution to satisfy those needs and desires.

Once you bring clarity to your mind, the energy of your environment will follow. You just have to keep questioning relentlessly until you feel you have touched a sense of truth about yourself in any specific situation that bothers you.

WHEN TO TOSS, WHEN TO TREASURE

Many people like collecting specific items when they travel, for example, or are just drawn to certain items no matter where they go. Personally, I'm drawn to crystals; you might collect teacups or antique clocks. It is good to remember that these special collections can quickly become clutter, which happens for two reasons.

First, too many items in a small space will inevitably create clutter, even if you really, really like them all. If you live in a small space, rearranging and editing is necessary; otherwise, the space can easily get overwhelmed. Second, after time, we inevitably either lose interest in our collections or do not see them anymore. This point is when the energy becomes life-less and clutter comes into being.

Let's briefly look into the idea of displaying and saving

true keepsakes. What might look like clutter to some can be very valuable to others. In the process of clutter clearing, you will get to distinguish between clutter and objects of value, even when they look very similar. Once you realize that all the cute snow globes mixed with a lot of random stuff are actually dear to your heart and make you so happy, you will find a beautiful way to display them as a collection. Or, if the space does not allow, you will find a beautiful box to store them in and visit them from time to time, getting lost in their wonder.

It is very important to identify your true keepsakes. Asking yourself the right question about the feeling of the items and *why* you keep them will help speed up this process.

AND IT'S JUST THIS EASY

There is a brilliant clutter-clearing system that I successfully use with my clients and have shared with thousands of readers all over the world. It is fast, fun, easy, and full of energy. Here it is in a nutshell.

You need:
- Three big boxes or bags
- A timer
- Optional: Energy-giving elements, such as essential oils, an aromatherapy diffuser, vibrant music, crystals, fresh flowers, or a small flowering plant

Step 1: Label the three boxes with the following, respectively:
- ✳ YES (Keep)
- ✳ NO (Give away)
- ✳ DON'T KNOW

Step 2: Set the timer for a maximum of 30 minutes.

Step 3: Start the process.

Place your three boxes close to the area that you plan to declutter. Pick up an item and quickly, without much thinking, toss it into the proper box. It is important to keep a somewhat steady rhythm when you sort your items into the YES and NO boxes.

Your body will respond with very clear messages right away, so listen. When you feel delayed or confused—which very often happens in the process of clutter clearing—throw the item into the I DON'T KNOW box and keep the rhythm going. Don't stop, don't try to figure it out, don't go into stories; just place the confusing item in the I DON'T KNOW box and keep going.

Sometimes you might end up with most stuff in your I DON'T KNOW box; that's okay! You still did a great job because you did your best. This box should go to storage; make a note in your calendar to check on it after three to six months. If, when the time for review comes, you do not even remember what's in the box, give it away without opening. It's that easy!

I love this system because it saves so much time, it is easy to do, and it works brilliantly! Even if all you end up with is a filled I DON'T KNOW box, you've already started a very powerful process!

Know that the more you get rid of your clutter, the more you free up precious energy to flow toward the life you want to live.

It is important to keep the first few sessions to a maximum time of 30 minutes so that you finish while you are still full of energy and enthusiasm. I highly suggest that you celebrate after each session. This way you not only build up good associations with clearing clutter, but you also wisely manage your energy by looking forward to more clutter-clearing sessions.

JOE'S STORY

Joe was constantly battling fatigue and lack of enthusiasm every time he tried to relax in his media room/man cave/office. Even though he was clearly drawn there, after just a little while, he had no energy left. His only desire was to lie down and do nothing, but this felt draining instead of relaxing or nurturing.

As this room was the only space in his home where he could be by himself, Joe kept spending time there, feeling more and more tired. He liked the look of the space, but the feelings of exhaustion and low energy made him question this arrangement.

At the suggestion of a friend, Joe contacted me to help figure out what was happening. Here are the main culprits that we uncovered:

No fresh air: The room had stale air, as there was no way to open the windows, and the variety of items in the nearby storage space created an unpleasant scent in the air. The fact that the room had old carpet certainly did not help, either.

No natural light or proper indoor lighting: Joe liked the space because it was dark; he found it very calming. The curtains were never opened and there was just one floor lamp with a somewhat depressing light. While it is true that dark colors can be very calming and cocooning, it is important to keep the energy in dark spaces clear and fresh.

No life energy, colors, or art: The space had no life to it—no details such as family photos, a mirror to create more flow, or splashes of bright color. It was all very flat and stagnant.

Wall-to-wall metal shelving in the Health & Family area: The energy of the Health & Family feng shui bagua area is weakened and even damaged when there is a strong presence of either

Metal or Fire elements. In this case, not only was the big shelving unit made from metal, but it also contained a variety of metal tools.

Stagnant energy of clutter: Almost half of the floor in Joe's man cave was covered in old magazines and sports paraphernalia. All of those items were neither recently placed nor being used, so the energy created was depressing and stagnant. Note that feng shui–wise, having too many items on the floor inevitably lowers your energy, so try to have as little as possible lying on your floor.

A cluttered floor surface, the lack of natural light and fresh air, and the insufficient indoor lighting all contributed to very low and stagnant energy. No wonder Joe was feeling depressed after spending time there.

Here's what we did:

- Cleared out the clutter on the floor using the And It's Just This Easy (page 48) system
- Replaced the old carpet with wood flooring
- Bought a high-quality air purifier
- Installed several levels of full-spectrum lighting
- Displayed two big, high-energy art posters to activate the space: an image of lush waterfalls that Joe really liked and an image of a window with wide-open sky
- Incorporated a few brightly colored cushions and some family and travel photos
- Painted one wall in a soothing blue color to bring more lightness into the room

It took only a few short weeks for the process to get completed, and once it was done, Joe really looked forward to spending time in the room. The only drawback was that other family members started finding their way there, too!

THE SIX-WEEK CLUTTER REBOOT

The first step in your clutter-clearing process is to define all areas in your home that you really want to see clean and organized. In the following table there are six of them, but you might end up with as many as 10 areas or as few as two. Plan to spend a week clearing each area and define how many sessions a week are needed in order to achieve your goal.

By using the And It's Just This Easy (page 48) system, your clutter-clearing process can be easy and even enjoyable—especially when you start feeling the effects of living with little or no clutter.

Follow the example table to help define the state of clutter in your home, track your progress, and acknowledge the results. As mentioned before, do not forget to celebrate your clutter-clearing efforts!

Know that the more
you get rid of your clutter,
the more you free up
precious energy to flow
toward the life you
want to live.

ROOM OR AREA	CLUTTER SCORE 1–10	INTENTION	PROGRESS REPORT	HOW DOES IT FEEL
Garage	10	I want to clear enough space to make it look welcoming as well as to create a small wood-working area.	Woohoo! Made $250 on my old bike and found my lost skates and a few of my favorite sketchbooks.	It feels awesome! I finally have room to park the car and a space that I'm not ashamed to show others. I've also started creating a hobby space! Love it.
Entryway closet	8	A closet that has order in it, even with all the items that inevi-tably have to be here.	I'm pretty happy with the closet organizers I just pur-chased. They allow me to clearly see what I need to keep and what I can let go of.	I feel like I can breathe again! And I'm not ashamed of it when guests come over. It's just so much more welcoming in the whole entry area.
Bathroom under sink	10	To let go of constant chaos there.	Cleaned up a lot and found nice containers for the rest of the stuff. Took many supplies to the storage area as there is really no need for all of them to be in the bathroom.	I feel calm in the bathroom now, whereas before, there was a sense of agitation and even feeling stuck. Now it can actually start feeling like a spa instead of a mudroom!
Children's room	7	A room that has the energy of fun, joy, order, and creative beauty (within possibility, of course).	Removed many old toys! Found a way to display toys up on the shelf instead of on the floor.	It feels sweet and creative without feeling cluttered and stagnant. Kids love it more, too. It seems they are sensitive to the newly created energy.

ROOM OR AREA	CLUTTER SCORE 1–10	INTENTION	PROGRESS REPORT	HOW DOES IT FEEL
Living room	5	A comfortable, open, and cozy space to spend time with family and friends.	Cleared out all magazines, donated some books, cleared clutter from the two big shelves, and repositioned the furniture.	Love being here now; there is way more open and fresh energy while the feeling of coziness remains.
Home office	6	I want an energizing feeling versus a boring, stuck feeling in the space.	It took some time, but I looked through all the paperwork and organized it. Most of it I did not need anymore.	My office feels and looks so much lighter! All the stacks of paper were really bothering me.

Along with the visible clutter, there is a lot of energetic clutter and even chaos that we cannot possibly see with our eyes. Many feel it as an energetic residue of illness, trauma, or any strong emotions expressed in the space. Spending time in a space that has its walls saturated with low energetic residues can be quite damaging. The body will constantly fight this assault, thus weakening itself and having less energy left for healing and happiness.

Some basic space clearing on a regular basis is always recommended, especially if you know that your whole house or a specific room carries heavy energy. There are many space-clearing techniques that I describe in detail in my book, *The Healing Power of Smudging*, from clapping to toning to using singing bowls. One of the most popular energy-clearing techniques is smudging the space, along with burning natural incense often, and setting a clear intention.

This challenging energy can be especially detrimental if it is in your Health & Family bagua area or in your bedroom. Be sure to check and see that the Heart Center and the bedroom have the brightest, freshest energy possible.

Here are some of the easiest ways to clear the energetic clutter or heavy energetic residues:

Music: Play inspiring music often. It is best to choose melodies without words, unless the words are very positive and clear.

Candles: Fire purifies the energy, so I highly suggest using candles as often as possible in your home. Be sure to choose natural candles and let them to do their purifying job while also creating a sensual and healing glow.

Imagery: Find an especially happy and powerful image to elevate the energy of the room, something that will combat and rebalance the negative energetic residue present there.

It can be an awe-inspiring nature image, an image from a spiritual or religious path that inspires you, or just abstract art with vibrant, happy, and potent colors. You can also place symbols and visuals that resonate with your specific health goals, such as weight loss or simply feeling more love and joy.

Incense and smudging: Purify your space with natural incense or by smudging it regularly. Smudging is a native tradition of purifying the energy by burning sacred herbs. It is wise and respectful to say a prayer before you begin smudging. You can choose to buy a ready-made smudge stick or make your own by gathering sacred herbs, such as white sage, cedar, rosemary, and lavender, and tying them in a bundle. Once the bundle is dry, light the tip of the bundle, then gently wave the smudge stick in the air until the tip begins to smolder.

Walk around your space and let the smoke purify each and every area of your home. It is recommended to keep the windows open so that the stale energy can leave. You should also have a small container underneath your smudge stick to prevent burning herbs from falling onto your floor or furniture.

Create an altar: A good place for your altar can be your mantel, the top of your bookshelf, a side table, a small wall shelf, or even your windowsill. Any bagua area is good for your altar, though it will especially benefit the Health & Family area, the Heart Center, or the Helpful People area. You can choose to cover the surface with beautiful fabric and then place items with healing energy and special meaning, such as crystals, candles, sacred herbs, special photos, flowers, and images of sculptures of deities. Having an altar in your home will create a healing quality of energy that is filled with gratitude and blessings spreading throughout the house.

If you want to improve your vitality, have full access to your own innate healing energy, and enjoy true well-being on a daily basis, you must commit to clearing your clutter.

MINDFUL
PAUSE

4-SQUARE BREATH

Sit quietly.

Draw your mind inward.
Relax your face,
chest, and belly.

Breathe in for four counts.

Hold for four counts.

Breathe out for four counts.

Repeat six to ten times.

Read the affirmation
out loud three times.

AFFIRMATION

Aliveness is a sacred experience.

CHAPTER

5

Since we are focusing on health and well-being, I would like to address specific concerns that many people might be struggling with along with feng shui strategies to help alleviate them. Please note that this book can't diagnose or treat an illness; the intent is to support your intuitive wisdom to know how to access more life-force energy on a daily basis.

Specific WELLNESS CONCERNS

Since feng shui is part of the same body of knowledge as Chinese medicine, its approach to health and healing is similar: Energy flows via specific pathways, and when those pathways are blocked, illness can occur. For this reason, in feng shui there is a big focus on a free and harmonious flow of energy inside the house. Having blocked areas in specific bagua areas of your house can manifest as difficulties in the life areas connected to those bagua areas.

Thoughts and mind-set also play a big role in the manifestation of disease or imbalance, so keeping yourself happy and gently but honestly watching your thoughts can help you protect your physical vitality. Keeping your life force, or Qi energy, flowing smoothly is very important for your physical and emotional well-being.

Because your energy is deeply connected to the energy of your home, opening up the flow of Qi in your home is very helpful. This principle is where feng shui becomes a truly healing art. Unblocking is done in many ways, as illustrated in the cases that follow.

STRESS AND ANXIETY

Stress and anxiety have become very common and are approached as a given in today's world. However, it doesn't have to be that way. Left untreated, stress can considerably weaken the energy of the body and even lead to illness. Creating a nurturing, restorative home environment can do wonders for easing anxiety and can help you bounce back faster from busy or stressful episodes.

WHAT TO LOOK FOR

Clutter, visual chaos, and energetically blocked areas are the first things to look for in a home that promotes stress and anxiety.

Here are a few other culprits that feed on and maintain the energy of stress in your body:
- A cold and uninviting bedroom
- A metal bed
- A home office in the bedroom
- An unkempt kitchen
- A bathroom with stuck energy and no beauty
- Unfinished projects everywhere
- Poor lighting
- Too many dark colors

- Too much TV time that takes over the energy in the living room, especially if the TV is located in the Health & Family area
- A big fireplace in the Health & Family area
- Big metal decor features in the Health & Family area

SOLUTIONS

To reduce stress and anxiety, it's important to create more calm, clear, and open space in your home. Commit to clearing your clutter and allowing more fresh air and sunlight into your space. Watch as little TV as possible, as there is a lot of negativity invading your psyche even after a very short time of watching. If you do watch a lot of TV, understand that anything you see on TV can energetically take over your living room and your home. A TV is especially damaging in the bedroom.

If you have a big fireplace in the Health & Family bagua area, hang a big round or rectangular mirror above it. A creative composition of waving shapes is acceptable, too, as they represent the Water element needed there to extinguish the Fire element. Consider investing in a good indoor fountain and placing it in

MINDFUL PAUSE

4-SQUARE BREATH

Sit quietly.

Draw your mind inward.
Relax your face,
chest, and belly.

Breathe in for four counts.

Hold for four counts.

Breathe out for four counts.

Repeat six to ten times.

Read the affirmation
out loud three times.

AFFIRMATION

Through all seasons, I live in
wonder and gratitude.

the Health & Family area to bring more of the Water element to this area. Remove any excessive metal decor in the Heart Center bagua, as it weakens that area's energy.

Next, transform your bathroom into a soothing oasis—or at least a space you enjoy and where objects are put away instead of left on the counters or ringing the bath tub. Take baths, perhaps with candles or flowers nearby to complete the spa atmosphere.

Throughout the home, add some brighter colors and frame happy photos from your travels and other inspiring experiences. Go for layered lighting, such as a mix of ceiling, table, and floor lamp options. Air out your space often by opening doors and windows. If you can't, go for an air purifier or an ultrasonic aromatherapy diffuser.

Here are more solutions for easing stress and anxiety with feng shui:

- Transform your bedroom into a soothing, healing, and sensual haven.
- Get rid of your metal bed if you can; it is really bad feng shui.
- Relocate your home office if it is in your bedroom.
- Take time to create a nourishing, tidy kitchen without too many objects left on the counters.
- If you have unfinished projects, group them together in one area out of sight.
- Treat yourself to vibrant flowers and lush plants.
- Listen to calming music often.
- Find the balance between activity and stillness by meditating and exercising often.
- Breathe often and breathe deeply.

WEIGHT GAIN

There are many elements that contribute to carrying excess weight, from a passive lifestyle to the subconscious desire to suppress emotional turmoil with food. Fortunately, making some changes in your living space can support your emotional wellness in ways that make it easier to maintain a healthy weight. Whenever clients tell me they can't lose weight easily, I begin looking for the usual suspects.

WHAT TO LOOK FOR

These signs around your house might help open your eyes to the cause of extra pounds:

- An overly cluttered kitchen, fridge, and freezer
- A front door that can't open fully due to objects in the way
- Blocked or overfilled areas in the house, especially in the Health & Family area
- Clutter under the bed
- Overflowing closets
- A basement and garage full of clutter
- An energetically unsupportive bedroom
- Lack of the Water and Fire feng shui elements in your home decor
- Toxic home elements, such as mold, geopathic stress, or asbestos in old, cracking paint

SOLUTIONS

The first step is to take a very good look at your kitchen and do your absolute best to declutter, organize, and create beauty in it. Using a light blue color in the kitchen can help curb the appetite.

Transform your bedroom into an oasis of sensual cocooning and healing. Bring small fresh flowers into your bedroom often, as well as small, shiny, golden metal decor items. Your bedroom should make you feel safe, comforted, and restored.

Next, check that your front door opens fully and beautifully with plenty of space around it. Move out from the doorway and check that it's easy to walk through your home and that there's no clutter or cramped spaces, including in your basement, garage, closets, drawers, and other hiding places. There should be openness throughout your home.

Here are a few more feng shui tips to support you with maintaining a healthy weight:

- Do not store anything under the bed; you want the energy to flow freely and smoothly so it can nourish you at night with its flow.

- Add a Water feng shui element feature, such as a fountain, a bowl of water, or a big mirror, to your home decor.
- Have your home checked for toxic exposure, especially in the bedroom. You may wish to add an air purifier to ensure you breathe clean, fresh air as you sleep.
- If you have an exercise room or dedicated exercise space in your home, be sure to bring the best energy to it with bright colors, crystals, and plants so that you are drawn there and exercise regularly.

MINDFUL PAUSE

4-7-8 YOGA BREATH

Sit quietly.

Draw your mind inward.
Relax your face, chest, and belly.

Breathe in for a count of four.

Hold for a count of seven.

Breathe out gently
for a count of eight.

Repeat six to ten times.

Read the affirmation
out loud three times.

AFFIRMATION

I choose the energy I allow into my
space—from the furniture I buy to the
food I eat, the music I play, and the
people I spend time with.

LOW MOOD

We can all experience low moods from time to time. It is completely natural to feel this way, but it should be balanced with good moods. If you are feeling low often, it is worth checking to see if anything in your home feng shui is creating this feeling or contributing to it.

WHAT TO LOOK FOR

Here are several potential culprits that can trigger low mood:
- Dreary colors
- Old carpet
- Lack of natural light
- Old furniture bought at a thrift or antique store
- Cluttered surfaces
- Dark kitchen and dining room
- Cold, unkempt bathroom
- Too many items on the floor
- The energy of sadness throughout the home, especially in the bedroom
- Lack of fresh air
- Blocked Qi flow
- Too much noise
- So many items stored under the bed that air and light can't pass under it
- Broken things and unfinished projects
- Cluttered basement and attic
- An empty and ugly bedroom
- Lonely images in dark colors
- Geopathic stress in areas where you spend a lot of time
- Heavy energy in the house left by previous occupants
- Big TV screen overtaking the room
- Home office in the bedroom
- Lack of beauty

SOLUTIONS

Begin by assessing the colors in your home. Adding fresh white paint and bringing in bright colors by painting walls or adding art or textiles can be very helpful in changing mood issues. Do away with worn-out materials or broken or damaged items, such as old furniture that has had many owners and could retain negative energy imprints. Either fix or let go of broken things in your house.

Consider how to bring more beauty into your home—especially your bedroom—be it with art, fresh flowers, an image to elevate your heart, or a small pebble you picked up by the river. When you're working with depression or low mood, building an altar to display items that inspire you and serve as an offering to divine energy can be very healing. You'll also want to smudge and clear the energy in your whole home, especially in the bedroom. Do a deep space-clearing session, as described in Rituals to Sanctify Your Time and Space (page 108), to let go of the potentially negative energy of previous occupants.

Also helpful is replacing old carpet with wood floors. If that's not possible, consider placing a colorful rug over old carpet. Open up the Qi flow by creating flowing pathways and open

spaces in your home, and open up all windows daily to allow maximum natural light.

Here are other feng shui tips for boosting your mood:

- Clean up all your counter surfaces; there should be only a few items on them.
- Bring light, joy, and happy colors to your kitchen and your dining room.
- Warm up your bathroom with color and decorate it with spa-like decor to create a restorative atmosphere.
- Find a way to place all boxes and toys on a higher level than the floor.
- Limit the noise you are exposed to daily.
- Clear all clutter, especially in the bedroom, basement, and attic.
- Replace all lonely, dark images with images of happy love, exciting adventure, unlimited curiosity, kindness, laughter, or other positive things.
- Check your house for geopathic stress and take action accordingly. For example, if your bed is over an area with geopathic stress, you should reposition the bed.
- Limit your TV time, especially in the evening and early morning.
- Never have a TV in the bedroom.
- Open up the space under the bed.
- Remove all electronics from your bedroom. Even a small electrical alarm clock creates an electromagnetic field that is higher than the level that promotes health and well-being.

MINDFUL PAUSE

4-7-8 YOGA BREATH

Sit quietly.

Draw your mind inward.
Relax your face,
chest, and belly.

Breathe in for a count of four.

Hold for a count of seven.

Breathe out gently
for a count of eight.

Repeat six to ten times.

Read the affirmation
out loud three times.

AFFIRMATION

I keep the energy in my home clear
and vibrant with natural light, fresh
air, and beautiful music.

INDIGESTION

On an energy level, indigestion is often a sign of various life experiences being left unprocessed or undigested. Creating good energy in your house can certainly help you alleviate the symptoms of indigestion.

WHAT TO LOOK FOR

These are some of the issues that can contribute to indigestion:
- Areas in the home that feel unlived in and unloved
- Bad design and bad energy in the kitchen, or a kitchen that feels cold and unfriendly
- A dining room with stuck energy
- A lack of beauty, music, movement, and love in the home
- An overwhelming number of distractions in the home, from loud TV that is on most of the time to clutter or too many collections
- Narrow hallways with no light
- A lack of color
- An overall cold energy in the home
- A blocked center of the home
- A lack of Fire element decor, like candles, triangular shapes, images of fire, and the colors red, orange, and yellow

SOLUTIONS

Begin by bringing love and attention to each area of your home, trying not to ignore any parts of it. Pay special attention to your kitchen—make it clean, colorful, and happy. Focus on yellow, be it with art, wall color, or a beautiful electric appliance. Yellow has the energy to activate digestion.

Beautify your dining room and use it more often. Try to use your dining table only as a dining table and keep its surface open and clean. Bring in beautiful decor, play happy music, and love your home the best you can.

Consciously limit the number of distractions in your home. Watch less TV, clear the clutter, and consider repositioning or packing up some of your collections.

Here's what you can do next:

- If you have narrow hallways with no light, repaint them in a color of your choice and hang art on both walls along with some small mirrors. If you can, bring good lighting to them.
- Color, color, and more color is needed in this case, especially the saturated richness of yellow.
- Warm up your home with textiles and other decor items in pleasing designs and colors.
- Open up and create beauty in the center of your home.
- Focus on Fire energy in your home decor, meaning items with triangular and star shapes, images of fire, an actual fireplace and candles, and the colors red, purple, yellow, magenta, and pink.

MINDFUL
PAUSE

4-SQUARE BREATH

Sit quietly.

Draw your mind inward.
Relax your face,
chest, and belly.

Breathe in for four counts.

Hold for four counts.

Breathe out for four counts.

Repeat six to ten times.

Read the affirmation
out loud three times.

AFFIRMATION

I honor Mother Earth, who blesses
my journey with vibrant,
healing foods.

FATIGUE

All of us experience fatigue at one point or another, no matter what our lifestyle is. Pressing deadlines, travel, family circumstances, and even too much fun can all lead to fatigue. However, if the fatigue lasts and you do not feel supported or have your energy replenished in your home, then it is time to take a closer look at your home environment.

WHAT TO LOOK FOR

These factors can create an excess of fatigue:
- Areas with geopathic stress, especially in the bedroom
- Too many electronics in the bedroom
- High levels of electromagnetic fields throughout the house
- Toxic areas in the basement, attic, bedroom, and kitchen
- A blocked front door
- Closets that are stuffed to the brim
- Crowded area under the bed
- A metal bed frame
- Lack of fresh air
- Lack of natural light
- Dark, dreary colors
- Too much furniture
- Clutter everywhere, even if it is hidden
- A bathroom that is unpleasant to be in
- Blocked energy in the kitchen

SOLUTIONS

Begin by checking your home, especially your bedroom, for geopathic stress. Remove all electronics from the bedroom. Limit the electromagnetic field levels in the house, especially at night. For example, turn the Wi-Fi router off. Check for any toxic emissions in the basement, attic, bedroom, and kitchen.

Next, move down this list, testing these changes and monitoring your energy levels:

- Open up your front door area and make it beautiful.
- Clear out your closets and create some space in them.
- Remove any items from under the bed.
- Let go of the metal bed.
- Aerate your home often.
- Allow maximum natural light.
- Lighten up your home with a fresh coat of paint and bright colors.
- If you have too much furniture in your home, either reposition, relocate, or let go of some pieces.
- Clear out your clutter, especially from the hidden pockets.
- Create a spa feel in your bathroom.
- Open up and nourish your kitchen, and create a sense of beauty in it.

MINDFUL PAUSE

4-SQUARE BREATH

Sit quietly.

Draw your mind inward.
Relax your face,
chest, and belly.

Breathe in for four counts.

Hold for four counts.

Breathe out for four counts.

Repeat six to ten times.

Read the affirmation out
loud three times.

AFFIRMATION

I create a home that nourishes
my energy and brings
healing pleasure to all my senses.

LONELINESS

Loneliness is a widespread feeling in our modern society as well as a frequent cause of depression. Good feng shui in the home can definitely help alleviate the feelings of loneliness and help you make your energy more available for social connection, friendship, or romance.

WHAT TO LOOK FOR

Here are a few culprits that increase feelings of loneliness:

- A home that doesn't feel beautiful to you
- A home that you have not made into a home yet, so it cannot support and befriend you
- Lack of color, sweet decor touches, and comfortable furniture for the body and mind to relax and soften
- Lack of natural elements, such as plants, flowers, crystals, and candles
- An imbalance of feng shui elements in decor—such as too much Water or Metal and not enough Fire, Wood, and Earth decor

- A lonely feeling in the bedroom or an imbalanced bed
- Lonely images throughout the house
- A front door aligned with the back door or a back wall with overly large windows
- A cold and unkempt basement
- Old carpet
- A mostly gray color palette
- A lack of books and photos of family and friends

SOLUTIONS

If you've been feeling lonely lately, take a good look at the coziness in your home. Make your place as warm, comfortable, and loveable as possible, no matter how long you plan to live there. Define what beauty means to you and bring it into your home. Bring color and small decor elements to warm your home. Soften up the look of your furniture and your room with more pillows, a new rug, or intimate lighting. Decorate with plants, flowers, crystals, or candles, or consider investing in a good fountain to activate the energy and make it more vibrant. Bring the elements that are most needed when one feels lonely: Fire, Wood, and Earth.

A balanced bed is a bed that has enough space on both sides for energy to flow and nourish you as you sleep. In addition, using similar nightstands and lighting on both sides promotes balance in a relationship, allowing partners to feel equally respected. If you are single, balancing your bed in this way fosters receptive energy and reinforces within your own energy field that you're open to a relationship and could welcome another.

The basement is the energetic foundation of a home, so be sure your basement is clean and organized. Check your basement and see what you can reasonably do there in order to create the solid energy of grounding.

Find a feng shui cure for the direct alignment of the front door with the back door or a wall with large windows. Leaving a direct alignment untreated can contribute to a major loss

of incoming Qi, which will weaken the energy of the house. A good example of keeping the Qi in is a masterful positioning of furniture, such as a round table or a grouping of plants in the pathway between the two doors.

Finally, use essential oils to evoke the feeling of happiness. Orange blossom, lemon, grapefruit, peppermint, cinnamon, lavender, and other essential oils can promote a vibrant and happy quality of energy in your space.

Here are a few more ways you can lift up the energy in your home to welcome more time with friends and loved ones or to help you meet new people and forge meaningful new friendships:

- Remove old carpet and replace it with wood floors.
- Add splashes of vibrant color throughout your home.
- Display books with happy titles and frame your favorite photos of family and friends.

MINDFUL PAUSE

4-7-8 YOGA BREATH

Sit quietly.

Draw your mind inward.
Relax your face,
chest, and belly.

Breathe in for a count of four.

Hold for a count of seven.

Breathe out gently for a count
of eight.

Repeat six to ten times.

Read the affirmation
out loud three times.

AFFIRMATION

I value and cultivate true friendships.

INSOMNIA

No matter how it is defined—not sleeping the whole night, not being able to easily fall asleep, or waking up in the middle of the night without falling back to sleep—insomnia can be very hard on one's body, mind, and emotions. Let's see how a good feng shui home can help you enjoy a full night's sleep.

WHAT TO LOOK FOR

Naturally, we begin with the bedroom. How does this room make you feel? Is it cold, cluttered, or unfriendly? Do you have a TV in your bedroom? That's a feng shui no-no, as a TV pours all kinds of energy into your sleeping space. Just think of the dramas and heavy news that could stream from it. Also evaluate the level of beauty in the room. Clear cluttered surfaces and remove or tidy anything stored under the bed. Ideally you should have nothing there except light and air. Finally, does your furniture have a lot of sharp edges? Sharp corners pointing at you while you sleep or beams above your head will hamper deep sleep.

Check the images around your house for sad or heavy scenes. Having too much or too little color could also affect your stimulation level and feelings of calm.

Here are a few more sleep blockers:
- Too many windows in the bedroom, especially if they extend across a whole wall
- Electronics in the bedroom
- Watching TV before bed
- Lack of beauty or nourishment in the bedroom as well as throughout the home
- Lack of comfortable areas in the home
- An unkempt bathroom

SOLUTIONS

Begin by visually warming up your bedroom with color and soothing images. Clear the clutter in your bedroom, especially under the bed. Reposition the furniture so that there are no sharp corners pointing at you while you sleep, or cover them at night. Bring beauty and nourishment to your bedroom and your whole home. Create at least one comfortable area in your home where you can cozy up with a book during a sleepless night.

Love your whole home so it can support you during sleepless nights and remind you to breathe deeply, softly, and steadily. Inspirational quotes, such as "This too shall pass" or "You are loved," can bring much comfort when your mind is racing due to lack of sleep. Make your kitchen welcoming at night to make some tea. Sit down on your comfortable sofa with gentle lighting nearby and a good book to read, or lie on a warm rug to do yoga. Plants and flowers can make for beautiful energetic nourishment and sweet company at night, so be sure to create your nighttime cozy space in a very loving way.

Try these tips, as well, and monitor your sleep quality as you make changes:

- Create a canopy to lessen the effect of a beam over your bed.
- Go for good window treatments if you have many windows in the bedroom, especially if they are across a whole wall.
- Remove all electronics from the bedroom.
- Do not watch TV or use any electronics before bed.
- Use soft lighting at night.
- Clear clutter and open up all surfaces.
- Create a spa feeling in your bathroom.
- Remove any and all images that create distress.
- Find a balance of colors in your decor. Avoid a fully monochromatic color scheme or too many bright colors.
- Have soothing elements in your bedroom that you can count on when you cannot sleep: an aromatherapy diffuser with calming scents, a crystal to hold, a soft blanket to cocoon in, or relaxing music.

CAMILLA'S STORY

Camilla started experiencing sleepless nights when she came back after a long trip and rented a new apartment. She postponed decorating it as she was still recovering and needed time to rest, but her sleeping patterns were not getting better. She also became more anxious in her new place, which she did not experience even during her challenging trip. Tired after so many sleepless nights, she finally decided to take care of herself and her new home.

At the suggestion of a friend, she started with some space clearing. Oddly enough, her new neighbors shared that the person who had lived there before tended to display aggressive behavior. This information helped her understand why she felt so anxious, so she decided to clear the space regularly. She left beautiful music on, smudged in the morning and at night before bedtime, and burned incense at her small altar in the bedroom. In time, she started feeling more at home in her new apartment and created a cozy space in the living room that was a pleasure to be in. It was surrounded with plants, a multicolor lamp, stacks of books, and a side table with many happy photos.

Camilla's bedroom underwent a complete makeover. She bought new bedsheets and upholstery, new window treatments, a gorgeous new rug in warm colors, and several beautiful floral pillows. She had an aromatherapy diffuser right by her bed spreading lavender essential oil into the air and used beeswax candles before going to sleep.

Her sleeping patterns did not improve overnight, but she noticed how much steadier, more supported, and calmer she felt even with just a few hours of sleep. Eventually, Camilla started sleeping through the night and feeling very grateful for it. She also found a best friend in the home that she so lovingly created to help her with overcoming insomnia.

MINDFUL
PAUSE

4-SQUARE BREATH

Sit quietly.

Draw your mind inward.
Relax your face,
chest, and belly.

Breathe in for four counts.

Hold for four counts.

Breathe out for four counts.

Repeat six to ten times.

Read the affirmation
out loud three times.

AFFIRMATION

It's okay not to know
where to go next. I trust life.

CHAPTER

6

Knowing how to take care of ourselves on all levels—physical, mental, emotional, and spiritual—is a crucial part of our journey. It is not a luxury, an indulgence, or a desire but an expression of maturity and responsibility. Genuine self-care is a key part of a regular routine and not something to be enjoyed from time to time or on special occasions.

Ongoing
SELF-CARE

Our health depends on the fragile balance of many interconnected levels, from physical to spiritual. When one level is out of balance, the other levels will inevitably reflect this imbalance, too. Developing the skill of staying attuned to your body allows you to take the right action at the right time. Self-care extends from nourishing massages to taking charge of one's finances, so it is a complex process that needs to be applied according to one's situation.

There is an incredible variety of healing modalities available today to help us reach and maintain optimum states of well-being. Many self-care techniques and tools, such as yoga, acupuncture, and meditation, have a very long history of use, and others are relatively new.

Self-care does not necessarily imply spending money; sometimes it is a simple act that makes a big difference. Taking a long
walk in the woods or choosing to spend a day in silence does not
cost anything other than the effort to make time for it. A warm
bath, a good heart-to-heart talk with a close friend, journaling,
and making time for healing intimacy, meditation, or dance are
all actions that depend only on our willingness to take them.

ENERGY WORK AS A WAY OF LIFE

Everything around us is made of Qi, including our bodies, so it is a good idea to regularly check how the energies around us influence our own energy. If you feel like your home is not supporting you, if you do not sleep or eat well, if you experience negative emotions, or if you notice an overall decline in your well-being, take a look at what is happening in your house on both the visual and energetic levels.

All the processes we discussed in this book—from space clearing and decluttering to specific feng shui element cures—need to be revisited from time to time, especially when there is a big change in the air. This change can be a change of seasons, a change of jobs, or something more subtle, like transitioning to a different stage in your life. It can also be a change that is hard to put a finger on but nevertheless is there.

Clutter is easy to see, so be sure to use the And It's Just This Easy (page 48) system whenever any area of your home starts accumulating clutter again. Energetic chaos is harder to notice, as you might not be able or willing to sense it. This is why I always recommend major space-clearing sessions at least a few times a year, with basic space-clearing sessions each week. This way, the energy is maintained at good levels and you do not end up with too much negative residue.

Once the clutter clearing and the energy clearing are set in motion and done on a schedule, your feng shui cures and adjustments will work much better. Simple feng shui cures, such as red color decor in the Fame & Reputation area or a bowl of rose quartz crystals in the Love & Marriage area, need to be regularly refreshed, repositioned, or cleansed in order to avoid becoming stagnant or inactive.

SEASONAL CHANGE

The change of seasons asks for a gentle and welcoming acceptance of the inevitable—what has been is gone and what is coming is a complete unknown. We usually prepare for the change of seasons in quite predictable ways. We tuck away the items from one season and slightly change the decor in our homes to match the upcoming season. We get excited for the summer and prepare to cocoon in the winter. We feel soothed when we follow familiar rhythms because of the sense of peace and belonging that they offer.

Each new season is the expression of the death of the old and the beginning of the new, so it is wise to enter it with a clear space and a clear mind. Doing so allows us to honor and fully release the old, thus welcoming the new season by being fully present. A few clutter-clearing sessions if needed, good organization and space clearing, and a basic seasonal ritual can make all the difference in fully living the new season of your life. Simple self-care steps, such as journaling, meditation, long baths, and long walks in nature, can help us ground our energies and become more present.

WHEN SOMETHING FEELS OFF

There are many ways an imbalanced quality of energy will express itself. Sometimes you know exactly what is happening and what feelings specific events triggered in you, and sometimes there is just no way to pinpoint the source of your discomfort. It is important not to overlook these times just because the reason for your experience is unknown. Trust and listen to your body because it has access to wisdom that the rational mind is not able to explain. Be present with the feelings that are going through your body.

When something feels off, instead of questioning or analyzing it, it is best to focus on moving the energy in your body and releasing it. Somatic, or body-based, practices can be used to help you move, release, and transform the questionable quality of energy. You might choose to go for a deep-tissue massage, a free-flow dance class, or something more complex, such as a Rolfing session. The key is to work with your body in order to release and transform the energy you are experiencing instead of analyzing it.

Performing a simple space-clearing ritual when something feels off is part of a good self-care routine. You could begin by smudging your room with sage or palo santo, a type of South American wood known for its purifying and mood-lifting properties. Other ways to clear energy include playing healing music, diffusing purifying essential oils, and lighting a candle while setting an intention. These are all simple space-clearing steps to help cleanse the energy and bring it back to peace and harmony.

When you feel overwhelmed, sad, fearful, or in any way imbalanced after a life change, it is important to spend time caring for yourself and your space.

AFTER A LIFE CHANGE

When you feel overwhelmed, sad, fearful, or in any way imbalanced after a life change, it is important to spend time caring for yourself and your space in order to welcome a healing and soothing energy. There are two areas in your home that are important to pay attention to when you are going through life changes: your bedroom and your living room.

Create a cocooning energy in your bedroom by bringing in soft textiles, using natural candles, playing soft music, treating yourself to natural bedsheets, and using comforting essential oil scents.

Ground the energy in your living room by decorating it with items that bring a heavier presence, such as a big bowl of crystals, neat stacks of books, or a tall lamp or statue.

Be sure to take good care of yourself during this time by creating a ritual you can apply for a set number of days, all depending on your intention. This can be as simple as lighting a candle every night for 21 days and saying your prayers and journaling every day about your feelings and intentions.

After a big life change, you are in the process of preparing the ground for what is to come, so be gentle with yourself. Believe in the best possible outcome, and always leave room for mystery.

LOOKING FOR A NEW HOME

When you are looking for a new home, it is important to create a fresh and clear quality of energy in your present home. Find some time to do a good space-clearing session so that the energy gets brighter and ready to attract and allow the change you are looking for. Move your furniture a bit and reposition selected decor details to create an overall feeling of lightness and ease. If you have too many items in your home, pack them and take them to storage. You will be packing soon anyway for your move!

Create an altar that shows what you want in your new home and expresses gratitude for already receiving it. On the altar, place the list of your desired things in the new home along with some images of homes that you like. The Helpful People bagua area will empower such an altar the most. Place a metal bell or a small metal chime on your altar and ring it often. Candles are always an excellent addition to any altar, and so is an image of a deity you love and feel devotion to. On this altar you can also place photos of people who have considerably helped you this lifetime. Doing so can help facilitate the same helpful energy in your process of finding a new home.

COMPLEMENTARY PRACTICES

Ancient people knew one simple truth: A good flow of Qi in the physical body leads to good health. Over centuries, people have developed a variety of methods to help cultivate one's Qi for longevity and vitality. Some of these methods, such as acupuncture, need to be performed by a practitioner, but many popular practices, such as Tai Chi, Qigong, and facial Gua Sha, can be done by yourself once you learn the basics.

There is a wide variety of time-proven modalities that you can use to improve your health and well-being; the right choice comes down to your preference, your time, and your budget. I encourage you to keep exploring different modalities until you find the one that works best. Once you find it, you should practice it regularly. It is not so much the variety of the modalities you practice but rather the consistency in practicing them that will bring you beneficial results.

Let's look at a few of the most popular healing modalities that share the same ancient Taoist healing roots as feng shui. I want to dive for a bit into the healing practices of acupuncture, Gua Sha, Tai Chi, and Qigong.

ACUPUNCTURE

The field of acupuncture is ancient and vast. It is about improving one's health by inserting tiny needles into specific points (called acupoints) on specific energy pathways in the body (called meridians). When a meridian or a Qi pathway is blocked, the organ that is connected to this meridian becomes blocked, too, which can trigger potential illness and an overall imbalance. Acupuncture is used to reawaken the body's capacity to heal itself and has been proven to have beneficial effects on all body systems, from the nervous system to the digestive system. It is successful in treating many imbalances, such as insomnia, asthma, lower-back pain, headache, and various addictions and emotional disturbances.

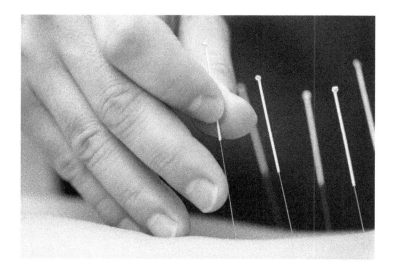

In addition to general acupuncture, there is also the field of umbilical acupuncture, where the practitioner works only with the umbilical area in order to influence the energy of various parts and organs of the body. There is also hand acupuncture, scalp acupuncture, and ear acupuncture.

When I had some minor health complications in New Zealand, a friend of mine recommended an acupuncturist. I was a bit skeptical. I had tried acupuncture before, but it was for overall vitality and rejuvenation purposes; there was nothing specific or obvious to heal. This time was different. I was in pain. Still, I went to see the acupuncturist and was very surprised when, after just minutes with a few needles in my earlobes, I felt a sense of deep calm and relaxation. By the next morning, I was fully healed and my symptoms were all gone! This experience demonstrates how accurate and powerful the ancient science of acupuncture can be. I am in awe and feel much gratitude every time I think of the wisdom of old Taoist masters and their laser-like visionary healing abilities.

GUA SHA

Gua Sha is an ancient Chinese healing technique in which the skin is scraped with short or long strokes in order to stimulate the circulation of Qi flow in the body. It is mainly performed on one's back, buttocks, neck, arms, and legs by using a specific wide-base tool. This ancient technique is believed to be a good solution to relieve the symptoms of a variety of conditions, such as headaches, neck pain, inflammation, perimenopause, arthritis, and more.

Even though many people try to do Gua Sha by themselves, this procedure is best performed by practitioners of traditional Chinese medicine. One of the risks associated with Gua Sha is skin bruising and possible minor bleeding because of rubbing and scraping the skin, so it is recommended to find a practitioner that has the proper certification and skills.

Facial Gua Sha is becoming very popular and is a procedure
you can easily do by yourself. Its main purpose is the same: to
unblock stagnant Qi and release toxins. Of course, the pressure
applied to one's face and neck is very light and gentle compared
to the whole-body Gua Sha procedure. The lymph drainage tool
used for facial Gua Sha comes in many beautiful crystals, from
rose quartz to jade, and is a pleasure to use.

TAI CHI

Tai Chi means "the supreme ultimate, the source and origin of
all life." It is visually expressed as the Tai Chi or the Yin Yang
symbol. Note that the *Chi* in Tai Chi is not *Qi*, as energy, but
rather *Ji*, for "the ultimate."

Tai Chi involves the application of the five elements, the
awareness of one's breathing, and slow movement as well as
the focus on calming the mind in order to achieve clarity and
ease. There are five major styles and many new variations of this
complex art. Tai Chi movements are relaxed and slow; they are

focused on the development of inner power and are not dependent on muscular tension.

The repetition of slow Tai Chi movements relieves the effects of stress on one's body and mind and promotes health and vitality. Focus, calm, and optimum health are the effects of consistent Tai Chi practice. Practicing Tai Chi every morning helps one stay healthy and happy.

There are many forms of Tai Chi. The longest one is the 108 movement form, and the shortest is the 24 movement form. The names of many Tai Chi forms are very poetic, including A Thousand Piece Brocade, Needle in Cotton, Grasp the Bird's Tail, and Quan Yin Tai Chi.

One of the main philosophies of Tai Chi is to meet violent force with softness rather than hardness. This applies to both physical and nonphysical force. A sign of Tai Chi mastery is the ability to follow the movement of an attacking force by remaining in physical contact with it until this force exhausts itself

or can be safely redirected. In many ways, Tai Chi is considered a superior martial art that takes years to master. I remember watching a documentary about a Tai Chi master in his 70s who easily and effortlessly defeated a physically strong and robust practitioner in his 30s. It was amazing to watch as it shows that Tai Chi is rooted in a deeply developed inner awareness and power rather than in reliance on physical strength.

QIGONG

Qigong is one of the oldest forms of energy work in ancient China. *Qi* means energy and *gong* means work. This healing art has been practiced for thousands of years and is used as a martial art as well as for healing and spiritual growth purposes. There are many benefits of Qigong, including a stronger life force, calmness, increased willpower, stress release, relaxation, and a sense of inner harmony. Considered part of a standard medical approach in China and used for the treatment of a variety of diseases from diabetes to cancer, Qigong cultivates one's life energy in order to promote health and longevity.

Qigong is powerful energy work that opens up the flow of Qi in all 12 major meridians as well as its smaller channels. It helps rebuild low levels of personal Qi, eliminate the blocks in its flow, and correct all imbalances. Qigong's gentle and slow movements are generally repeated and performed with deep rhythmic breathing and a calm state of mind. This practice increases the movement of fluids throughout the body and improves one's balance, strength, flexibility, and body awareness.

As proof of the power of Qigong, look to the story of a Qigong practitioner named Li Ching-Yuen from the Sichuan province in China. He was believed to be close to 200 years old at the time of his death. It sounds incredible, but there is actual documentation about his life when he passed away in the early 1900s.

There are literally thousands and thousands of forms of Qigong, so how do you choose which form to practice? The advice is to first find a teacher that you resonate with, because the transmission from the teacher is important in establishing the right practice. The most popular basic forms of Qigong are the standing forms called the Eight Pieces of Brocade Qigong and the Dragon and Tiger Qigong.

Learning to stand tall like a tree and to strengthen the energy in your legs, maintain structure, and relax within this structure are the first steps in successful Qigong practice. Understanding the alignment of your body and learning proper stance, good breathing, and a relaxed awareness are all conducive to successful results.

Qigong movements might look simple and easy to follow, but there is a wealth of knowledge about health and vitality behind each graceful movement. Called a moving meditation, the foundation of a good Qigong practice is built on proper alignment and correct belly breathing. These elements allow the practitioner to relax, get into a meditative state, and become more attuned to the flow of Qi in his or her body.

Here's a simple Qigong sequence to help awaken your Qi. This movement is good to do before a longer Qigong session or

Stand straight with your feet parallel, and shoulder width apart. Your knees should be slightly bent, and weight distributed evenly on both feet. Your chest, belly, shoulders, and arms are relaxed with armpits slightly open. Take a few deep breaths and relax.

Bring your hands together in front of your lower Dantien (the "sea of Qi" located two inches below your navel), palms facing the sky, fingertips close but not touching.

Breathe in and slowly raise your hands to your heart (called the middle Dantien) feeling the upward movement of energy.

when you need a quick way to calm and balance your energy during the day. The rhythmic movement helps clear the mind and gently strengthens your energy.

4

Breathing out, turn your palms to face the ground and bring your hands back to the lower Dantien. Repeat 8 to 16 times, moving slowly and with a gentle focus on your breath and sensing both the upward as well as the downward movement of energy.

5

When complete, take a minute or so to stand still and feel the energy in your body and mind getting more balanced and calm.

There are many benefits of Qigong, including a stronger life force, calmness, increased willpower, stress release, relaxation, and a sense of inner harmony.

RITUALS TO SANCTIFY YOUR TIME AND SPACE

Rituals are a time-proven way to honor the sacred, express gratitude, and set intentions for the welcoming of new creations in one's life. Humans have been using rituals for a very long time as an energetic support for empowered and harmonious living.

Given that feng shui is all about the interconnectedness of energies around us, this book would not be complete without rituals for your home to help shift and heal your personal energy. Performing a ritual in your home is bound to help change your energy, because your personal energy is deeply connected to the energy of your home.

We go through a wide variety of experiences in our lives, and while we can't have a ritual for each experience, certain ones need our attention. Performing a simple ritual for these experiences helps us cleanse and release the energy, tie loose ends, heal, and move on. When we do not stop to acknowledge and honor specific events in our lives, we become overburdened with

too many unresolved energetic residues burdening our psyche. Over time, this burden can become a major source of stress and discomfort.

GRIEF-HEALING RITUAL

There are three steps that need to happen in order for any healing to occur:

1. Acknowledging that we are grieving by clearly bringing it to the forefront of our awareness. For example, we may become aware that we are still grieving the loss of our marriage.

2. Allowing the process to unfold by feeling it rather than suppressing it and by analyzing its content. In this case, we are willing to let all these feelings run their course: "I feel sadness, grief, regrets, anger. This is so hard, but I know that this, too, shall pass. I need to feel it in order to heal it."

3. Accepting and receiving all the help we need in order to heal. "I know I can do this by myself, but if it gets too hard, I am willing to ask for all the help that is available to me, from close friends and family to a good therapist."

When you are going through this process, it is helpful to create an altar for grief and express what you are grieving and your feelings. Find visuals that support the full expression of your experience. In the process of grieving, many of us tend to repress our feelings, so create this altar as a reminder to tend to your feelings.

Emphasize the flow of the Water element in your grieving altar, because this element facilitates the process of release and healing. To do so, place a small bowl with fresh water that you change daily, or set up a beautiful fountain. If these options are unavailable, you can place a photo of fresh streams of water, waterfalls, rivers, or oceans. For this specific ritual, be sure to avoid images of still water, such as lakes.

Go to your altar as often as needed, and find ways to express your grief while there. For example, you can choose to record your voice expressing what you are going through at the moment, to journal, or even to express your grief in an impromptu song. You can also choose to move your body in specific ways in order to release the waves of grief. Or maybe your medicine will be stillness and meditation.

It is best to perform this ritual midway between a full moon and new moon. Express gratitude for the healing that is happening; pray for those who are going through the same process. Choosing to light a candle at your altar every night for 21 or even 40 days can be of powerful help.

ANCESTOR BLESSING RITUAL

Blessing and honoring our ancestors is a sacred process. We are all part of a specific lineage, and honoring this lineage, with all its complexity, is a responsibility that can bring many blessings. It is good for one's well-being to feel part of a specific lineage, as it can help provide more clarity about one's path and specific gifts.

There is another aspect to ancestor blessings that comes from feng shui. It is a little-known fact that feng shui started as the art of finding the best land formations for burials. Traditionally, Chinese people believed that an angry, disrespected ancestor could bring much misfortune to the family, so the best efforts were put into honoring them.

Your ancestor blessing ritual can be simple or elaborate; it all depends on your intent. In each case, the first step is to create an altar to honor all your ancestors by displaying some of their photos, writing down your blessings, lighting a candle, and playing quiet music. The best feng shui bagua areas to place your altar in are the Heart Center of your home and the Health & Family area. An auspicious day to perform your ritual

can be determined by a specific day in your family lineage or by an overall auspicious day, such as a specific new moon.

Smudge your space and say a prayer for all your ancestors. Place healing crystals close to their photos. Find a creative way to express your blessings and connection to them, such as with a song, with a dance movement, or by creating a specific piece of art. Keep the energy of blessings in your awareness and conclude by writing a letter to all your ancestors. Place the letter on your altar and tend to this altar by lighting a candle each day for nine days.

CLEANSING RITUAL

Cleansing rituals should be part of the regular energetic maintenance of one's home and personal energy. They are more than space-clearing sessions because a ritual is a sacred container with a specific intent rather than a general cleansing. You might have a cleansing ritual connected to a recent conflict in the family, for example, or to clear the energy of a relationship that is important to you.

There are two feng shui elements that have the strongest cleansing powers: the Fire and the Water elements. We will use

these elements in our ritual. As always, start by creating an altar and finding the best place to display it, which will depend on its specific intent. For example, if you are cleansing the energy of a relationship, then the Love & Marriage area is the best place to display your cleansing ritual altar.

Smudge your space or light an incense stick if the energy feels heavy. Place a glass or a metal bowl filled with water (Water element) in the center of your altar and surround it with five red candles (Fire element) to energize your altar. Express your intent for specific cleansing and add a few drops of a purifying essential oil, such as frankincense, sage, or peppermint, to the water bowl. Use the water from the bowl to sprinkle all corners of your house while reciting a cleansing prayer that comes from your heart. Come back to your altar and place the bowl back in the center of the candle formation. Fill it with flowers. The best timing for a cleansing ritual is the full moon.

GRATITUDE RITUAL

You do not need to wait for a specific time or event to perform a gratitude ritual. Perform it as often you can, because expressing gratitude fills both your heart and your home with beautiful energy. This ritual, in turn, activates a wealth of prosperous and happy energy to flow into your life.

Creating an altar expressing the energy of bounty is always the best way to express the energy of gratitude. Make this altar permanent and display various items that carry your gratitude. Think about how you can express this energy visually on your altar. From photos of people and places to images of vibrant health, genuine love, or successful work; or from a beautiful crystal to a letter from a dear friend or the image of the sea that you love so much, these objects can help you use your altar to reinforce the presence of these energies in your life.

The gratitude ritual in itself is simple. Find a time when you will not be disturbed, and meditate in front of your altar, recalling all the things you are grateful for. Light a candle and say a prayer for such blessings. Pick up an item from your altar and place it in your bedroom to saturate the room with the energy of gratitude. Keep it by your bed until your next gratitude ritual, when you will pick up another item and place it in a different area of your home. In time, your whole home will be saturated with the beautiful energy of gratitude. Come back to your altar and write down your gratitude for specific things you intend to come into your life.

As the old saying goes, gratitude is the best—and only—attitude!

THANKS AND ENJOY YOUR JOURNEY

Thank you for joining me on this journey.

I trust you have found many helpful ideas that you are inspired to try and that you've begun a relationship with Qi energy and feng shui that will support you for life.

I encourage you to make a list of at least eight different changes that you can implement in your home, and observe how they improve your well-being. You do not have to wait for health complications in order to start implementing various suggestions in this book. A home with great feng shui is one of the best illness prevention strategies. Use your home to take care of yourself—and enjoy the process.

I also encourage you to define what beauty and inspiration mean to you and to allow this energy to bless and energize your home. This can be as simple as a bouquet of wildflowers or as complex as a grouping of tall crystal clusters; what is important is that you really feel uplifted and happy when surrounded by this energy.

Beauty is in the eye of the beholder, and beauty is healing. So define this energy and surround yourself with it. This is excellent feng shui and is soothing for your soul. After all, if your inner world is in harmony, everything else falls into place.

Enjoy working with the information in this book, and if you want to connect, feel free to reach me either via my websites or on social media. Many blessings on your journey!

WEBSITES

FengShuiSociety.org.uk
A wonderful source of information on feng shui courses, events, and consultants in Europe.

IFSGuild.org
A website full of information on feng shui courses, events, and consultants in North America.

KnowFengShui.com
A site with a variety of feng shui tips, an online store, and a weekly newsletter.

Mindbodygreen.com
A comprehensive health and wellness website.

WOFS.com
One of the earliest online feng shui journals.

BOOKS

Clear Your Clutter with Feng Shui by Karen Kingston
This book will help you understand the far-reaching effects of clutter and get motivated to clear it for good.

Feng Shui and Health: The Anatomy of a Home by Nancy SantoPietro
A thought-provoking book on the relationship between home decor and specific illness patterns.

The Healing Power of Smudging: Cleansing Rituals to Purify Your Home, Attract Positive Energy and Bring Peace into Your Life by Rodika Tchi
A comprehensive, full-color how-to on the ancient tradition of space clearing with sacred smoke.

Sacred Space: Clearing and Enhancing the Energy of Your Home by Denise Linn
This wonderful book will help you learn how to clear and enhance the energy of your home and transform it into a sanctuary.

The Western Guide to Feng Shui: Creating Balance, Harmony and Prosperity in Your Environment by Terah Kathryn Collins
A practical and easy-to-read book on applying simple feng shui changes in your home.

To Sophia, for her kindness, maturity, and huge heart of gold. You keep amazing me every day and my heart is full of awe and gratitude for this deep relationship.

To my many teachers and friends who help me grow, inspire me, and believe in me.

To the Callisto Media team, for making the whole process so easy and effortless: Wesley Chiu for finding me, Rochelle Torke for your sweetness and keen eye to detail, and Garrett McGrath for patience and professionalism.

To my extended family in Europe.

To you, holding this book; I trust you will benefit much from it.

To life that keeps teaching me how to show up. I'm still learning.

Thank you.

Rodika Tchi knows how to use feng shui to create vibrant, healthy, and beautiful spaces. She has consulted on both residential and commercial spaces in Vancouver, BC, Canada, and long distance, for over 19 years. Rodika has helped numerous clients create harmonious homes as well as apply feng shui to quickly sell houses or improve businesses.

Rodika taught feng shui at the University of British Columbia as well as Hollyhock, Canada's leading educational retreat center. She has been interviewed by *Elle Decor*, *Style at Home*, *Canadian Living*, *The Globe and Mail*, the *Miami Herald*, the *Investment Executive*, *Vancouver* magazine, *Business Insider*, and others. Her media appearances include CBC TV, City TV, Global TV, and Shaw TV.

CPSIA information can be obtained
at www.ICGtesting.com
Printed in the USA
JSHW050420200721
17023JS00005B/5